Rookie
biographies®

Rosa Parks
Revised Edition

By Wil Mara

Reading Consultant
Cecilia Minden-Cupp, PhD
Former Director of the Language and Literacy Program
Harvard Graduate School of Education
Cambridge, Massachusetts

Children's Press®
A Division of Scholastic Inc.
New York Toronto London Auckland Sydney
Mexico City New Delhi Hong Kong
Danbury, Connecticut

Designer: Herman Adler Design
Photo Researcher: Caroline Anderson
The photo on the cover shows Rosa Parks.

Library of Congress Cataloging-in-Publication Data

Mara, Wil.
  Rosa Parks / by Wil Mara.— Rev. ed.
    p. cm. — (Rookie biography)
  ISBN-10: 0-531-12451-7 (lib. bdg.)   0-531-12592-0 (pbk.)
  ISBN-13: 978-0-531-12451-2 (lib. bdg.) 978-0-531-12592-2 (pbk.)
  1. Parks, Rosa, 1913—Juvenile literature. 2. African American women—
Alabama—Montgomery—Biography—Juvenile literature. 3. African
Americans—Alabama—Montgomery—Biography—Juvenile literature.
4. Civil rights workers—Alabama—Montgomery—Biography—Juvenile
literature. 5. African Americans—Civil rights—Alabama—Montgomery—
History—20th Century—Juvenile literature. 6. Segregation in Transportation—
Alabama—Montgomery—History—20th century—Juvenile literature.
7. Montgomery (Ala.)—Race relations—Juvenile literature. 8. Montgomery
(Ala.)—Biography—Juvenile literature. I. Title. II. Series.
  F334.M753P38554   2006
  323.092—dc22   2006004643

CHILDREN'S PRESS, and ROOKIE BIOGRAPHIES®, and associated
logos are trademarks and/or registered trademarks of Scholastic Library
Publishing. SCHOLASTIC and associated logos are trademarks and/or
registered trademarks of Scholastic Inc.

1 2 3 4 5 6 7 8 9 10 R 16 15 14 13 12 11 10 09 08 07

Rosa Parks changed the world
in one day.

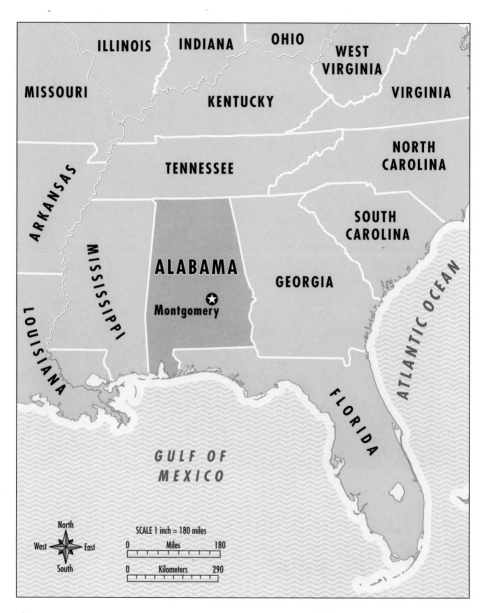

ILLINOIS INDIANA OHIO WEST VIRGINIA

MISSOURI KENTUCKY VIRGINIA

ARKANSAS TENNESSEE NORTH CAROLINA

SOUTH CAROLINA

MISSISSIPPI **ALABAMA** GEORGIA

⭐ Montgomery

LOUISIANA FLORIDA

ATLANTIC OCEAN

GULF OF MEXICO

North
West East
South

SCALE 1 inch = 180 miles

0 Miles 180

0 Kilometers 290

She was born Rosa Louise McCauley on February 4, 1913. She grew up in Alabama. Alabama is a state in the South.

Rosa was an African American.
The South was a difficult place
for African Americans to live.
It was a time when laws did not
give African Americans the same
rights as white people.

These laws said that African Americans could not go to the same schools as white people.

The laws also said they could not eat in the same restaurants or drink from the same water fountains. Rosa thought this was wrong.

On December 1, 1955,
Rosa was sitting on a bus
in Montgomery, Alabama.
Then a white man got on.
He wanted to sit in Rosa's seat.

African Americans were
supposed to give up their
seats to white people.

The bus driver told Rosa to get up. Rosa was tired of not being treated fairly. She said "no."

The police came and took her away to jail.

Three days later, Rosa went to court. She was fined fourteen dollars. She refused to pay the fine.

African Americans were angry about Rosa's arrest. They wanted the unfair laws changed.

On December 5, African Americans said they would not ride on any buses. This is called a boycott.

During the boycott, very few African Americans took buses in Montgomery. Most were empty.

A meeting was held in a
church in Montgomery.

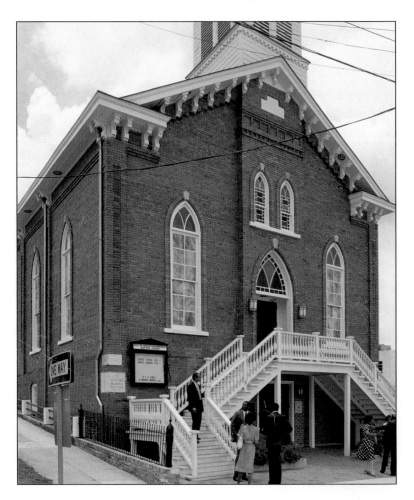

An African American minister told his people not to ride the buses until the laws were changed. The minister's name was Martin Luther King Jr.

African Americans walked or
rode in cars and taxis.

They did not ride the buses for a year. The bus companies lost a lot of money.

Finally, on November 13, 1956, the U.S. Supreme Court changed the law.

African Americans did not have
to give up their seats to anyone.

Rosa Parks kept fighting against the unfair treatment of African Americans. She traveled to many places and spoke to many people.

Millions were saddened by her death on October 24, 2005. She was 92.

Rosa Parks made life better for all African Americans by just saying "no."

Words You Know

African Americans

Alabama

arrest

boycott

Martin Luther King, Jr.

Rosa Parks

Supreme Court

Index

About the Author

Wil Mara has authored more than seventy books, both fiction and nonfiction, for children and adults.

Photo Credits

Photographs © 2007: AP/Wide World Photos: 3, 31 bottom left (Khue Bui), 12, 30 bottom (Gene Herrick), 15, 16, 22, 23, 25, 31 top left; Corbis Images: 19, 27 (Bettmann), 20, 21, 31 top right (Flip Schulke), 24, 31 bottom right (Joseph Sohm; Visions of America); Getty Images/Stan Wayman/Time Life Pictures: 11; Library of Congress: 8, 30 top left; Magnum Photos/Eli Reed: 29; Stockphoto.com/Black Star/Owen: 7; WireImage.com/Monica Morgan: cover.

Map by Bob Italiano